Backpacking Made Easier

Your Step-by-Step Guide

Mark James Vang

ISBN: 978-1-4834-0476-9 (sc)
ISBN: 978-1-4834-0478-3 (hc)
ISBN: 978-1-4834-0477-6 (e)

Library of Congress Control Number: 2013919890

Lulu Publishing Services rev. date: 11/13/2013

Dedication

With thanks to all those I've met on the road – you're an inspiration to why I travel. Thanks, too, to family, whom I've worried endlessly by going off continuously and to friends who've supported my decisions and kept in touch whilst on the road. I'm a product of all your love.

Acknowledgements

Thanks to Merete, Thomas and Mark for their invaluable input, support and advice. Without them, I would not have had the courage to complete the book.

Contents

Introduction

With the advent of the internet, travel has never been easier. When I first began traveling sixteen years ago, there were no internet cafes or wifi, communication was via phone cards and faxes, and mail was received via *poste restante* (a mail collection service offered by post offices). Nor was there a way of safeguarding your photos other than sending the rolled film home.

At the same time, however, the internet has complicated travel. People used to buy guidebooks, ask around for advice, and then simply book a ticket and set off. Search engines bring up blogs and travel forums with a proliferation of free information but they will often be subjective and sometimes contradictory. There are few places where all the information is consolidated or contains exactly what you need to know. Indeed, many blogs are skewed for commercial purposes with click-throughs and advertisements.

The purpose of this book is to manage the first-time backpacker's expectations, helping them to plan their trip and provide safety tips so that they return with everlasting memories.

Pre-trip planning and safety is a large proportion of this book because the *on the road* bit is actually pretty easy if you properly prepare. *Backpacking Made Easier*'s departure from other backpacking books is that it includes illustrated examples to aid budgeting and route planning, advice for how to back up your photos, and advice about the often-neglected psychological impact of returning home. There's also some personal tips you won't find in other guidebooks from someone who's traveled by varying methods – with a partner, with a friend, and solo; short trips versus long; and with a fixed itinerary versus on a flexible route. There are also top tips on guarding your belongings in accommodation and on transport. This is not an A–Z country guide – that information is available on the internet. It's *your* trip, so I'll help you plan how to follow your dreams!

Where I have italicized words, it is for emphasis. Where I have name-dropped countries, it's not for bragging rights – it's to help you visualize the places I have been that you may be considering. Your biggest asset while on the road is your gut instinct. You used it by purchasing this book. Don't let fear and inertia overcome you. Traveling is one of the most rewarding things you can do in your lifetime. You're just a few steps away. I'm excited for you!

Before You Go

Section 1

Planning

When done properly, planning ahead can magnify the enjoyment of your trip and doesn't need to be a chore. Part of the fun of planning is reading up about the places you want to visit. Planning should be broken down into research and trip planning (the fun part), including budgeting, vaccinations and health (easy, but requires time and organization), passports and visas (also easy), ticket and insurance purchase (go celebrate once booked!) and final preparations such as arranging finances and storage of belongings (the less fun part, but hey, you're almost off on your trip!).

To give yourself ample time, you need to start earlier than you think. For example, some courses of injections require three jabs with intervals between each. You may need to approach an estate agent to find a tenant or find someone to sublet your room and someone to accept your post if you redirect it, so starting *early* is the key.

First, let's get the burning questions out the way: Who do you meet, and why go? This can be the stumbling block for many first-time backpackers. It doesn't matter whether you're in school or employed; you're probably used to routine and a certain level of comfort, so not knowing what to expect can be intimidating. It also helps to work out early on whether to go alone or with someone else. For example, is budgeting and route planning a joint or sole decision?

Some advice for picking locations will follow on from this through an illustrated example. Going on your own simplifies planning, but it can have its upsides and downsides once on the road. Planning with someone else can be complicated. If at the planning point you already show differences in wants and goals, think twice before you hit the road.

Who Do You Meet and Why Go?

To the first-time backpacker, leaving the status quo and jumping into the unknown can be incredibly daunting. You've skimmed through guidebooks and got an impression, but you don't really know what to expect. Some aspiring travelers will allow inertia and fear to take over, and their planning will stop at the purchase of guidebooks. Others start a one-way journey; once you've backpacked, you just want to add more countries to the list! You'll meet people from all around the world who will tell you about where they've been, and you'll remember their stories when planning your next trip. If you take heed of the safety tips in this book and your guidebook, once you're there, you'll wonder what all the fuss was about and wish you'd gone earlier.

"So who will I meet?" and "Am I too young?" or "Am I too old for this?" Dispel your fears; age is not a barrier to travel. Generally speaking, you'll meet gap-year students (between high school and starting university), graduates (post-university), people on career breaks (sabbaticals, redundancies), people with a change of circumstances (in bereavement or recently separated), and semi- or full retirees. That's the whole age range from 18 to 60 and upwards. You'll be sleeping in the same places and doing day trips together, so it's not uncommon to travel with people from different backgrounds, from different countries and of differing age if you meet and get along. That's partly why you go traveling – to get away from the status quo!

But it's not just fellow travelers that make your trip. Locals can affect your trip just as much and in many cases more. A small percentage of travelers stay in their hostels, watch DVDs, and spend their time on Facebook or email. My suggestion: Get out there!

Some of my fondest memories are of spending time with restaurant owners who sat with me and played guitar long after closing hours, having tea and talks with shop owners, enjoying dinner in someone's house, and volunteering in a school or orphanage. Regardless of age, background, or nationality, people like to engage in discussion and banter. But respect the local culture, and don't forget to ask permission before photographing someone.

As a gap-year student or graduate, you'll learn how to budget better and become more confident and independent. Contrary to the thoughts of your parents (who are of a different generation that didn't travel), prospective employers like a candidate who is well-rounded, traveled, and mature, especially if they have worked (in part or full) to earn the money the trip required. It is also more satisfying to know you have raised the money. Of course, contributions from Grandma are welcomed!

If you worry about what your employer or future employer will think, you'll effectively be confined to a desk until you collect your pension. It *may* cost you a pay rise or promotion in the short term, but by carrying on disgruntled and unhappy, you may even be at risk of illness (mental or physical) or redundancy if your work deteriorates. That is why many companies encourage a sabbatical after three to five years. They've invested time and money in your training, so they don't want to lose you and go through the cost and effort of employing someone else. But at the same time, they recognise that people need time out to recharge their batteries. You'll be a happier individual after traveling, as it should change your perspective on work and life balance upon your return. Regardless of where you are in life, you'll have new friends across the globe!

Who Do You Go With?

Traveling with a friend or partner can be one of the most intense things you can do. It is a 24-hour-a-day commitment. You have to really know that person, as your relationship will be tested – *compromise* is the key word. It is quite important also that you are traveling on a similar budget. You'll be held back if you have a higher budget than your companion, and you'll be resentful if you have a lower one. On the other hand, if you have never traveled on your own before, the prospect can be quite intimidating and scary.

The latter option can in fact be the most rewarding, and you needn't be alone if you follow my basic tips. There will always be an excuse for a companion not going ("I have a wedding to attend," "I'm not sure I can afford it," "I don't think I am brave enough"), so don't rely on a friend. Just do it yourself. The timing won't ever be right for everyone, and you have limited times in your life (unless you make it a profession) when you will have chunks of time available to travel. Once you start working, you have limited annual holiday until you collect your pension. That's more scary! Better to take the opportunities while you can to take *months* off rather than *days*, no matter how intimidating taking that leap is. By going on your own, you often meet more people. Traveling with a friend or partner can be a barrier to people approaching you, as they assume you want to be left alone and you may not feel inclined to approach people.

Traveling with a Friend: It can almost be easier to travel with a stranger you meet than a friend. If your friend prefers beaches to cities and nightclubs to pubs, for example, a compromise is harder to reach, and you can both find yourself doing what you don't want to do. But you have no tie to a stranger and can always go in separate directions.

Sit down with your friend beforehand and discuss mutual objectives and things to see or achieve. Make sure to agree on the route. You will want space from each other at times (even if it is just for an hour), so your potential traveling partner should be a good enough friend that you won't offend them by saying, "I'm just going to sit in a cafe and update my diary for a while. I will see you later." Equally, they should be a good enough friend that you can say, "Why don't you head to the beach and we can meet back up in three days?"

After splitting up with a companion for a short while, you usually find that you miss each other even though you were annoying each other just a short period ago! If you don't think you and your friend will be compatible travel companions, don't set off together. You don't want to strain an important friendship. Remember, traveling is not just a holiday; you'll be sharing a room, getting night buses together and seeing habits you didn't know they had before (e.g., snoring – shared a room before?). You may also have to tolerate them finding a new *love*. Traveling together can strain a friendship but can also be incredibly rewarding; having a shared experience to look back on will often bring you closer. Practically, traveling with a friend means that you have another set of eyes to look after your belongings on the beach or at transport terminals. It can also be cheaper to share accommodation, and you have an automatic buddy for hiking or the pub.

Traveling with a Partner: Even though you perhaps live with your partner or spend most of the time around each other's houses, you typically have separate work lives and so will never have spent 24 hours a day together in a strange environment. A holiday can be wonderfully romantic, and you're not in each other's pockets. Traveling can be at times less romantic. There will be times when your partner is ill, tired, or grumpy from long journeys or early alarm clocks. And of course, third parties may get between you, such as an overly attentive hostel owner or hawker on the beach. You may find yourself having arguments you would never normally have. You have to be less harsh on each other and more forgiving. People can make mistakes. I have met many a couple who have started a trip together and ended it separately. Of course, if you survive your trip together, you can survive most things as a couple. You know that you have the foundations of a great future, and your shared experience will cement it further. If you know ahead of time that you will stick together through thick and thin, you can also divide items between you when packing and carry less weight.

Traveling Alone: One disadvantage of traveling alone is that you won't have someone to keep an eye on your bags if you need to go the bathroom in a bus station or in a restaurant. It is often more expensive getting a single room than a twin if you work out that dorm rooms aren't for you. You may have to round up numbers to go hiking (never go alone) or do activities, and getting a taxi or hired car without someone to share costs with can eat into your budget. You may feel self-conscious, for example, when eating in a restaurant without company (trust me, though: no one really notices but you, and it can be a good opportunity to update your diary, annotate your guidebook, or finish that chapter you started on the plane!). However, you need not ever be alone.

> Tip: For the first-time traveler, for your first destination, book your accommodation in advance. I suggest booking for two nights in a hostel that has a communal living area where you will meet people and that organizes daytrips. It may be cheaper to book through a travel agency in town (as you learn from experience), as the hostel will take commission.

But booking through the hostel is a great way to meet people who you may want to go for a drink with in the evening or travel onwards with to the next town. If there's somewhere you really want to go, ask anyone in the communal areas if they want to share a taxi or head out. If there are no takers, head out there anyway (see *Personal Safety* later) and ask a sociable-looking group whether they mind you joining. This seems easier said than done if you lack confidence or experience, but people are receptive to the solo traveler, as you are all in the same boat. Doing this a few times will build confidence, and before you know it, you'll be spotting lone travelers eating on their own and inviting them to join your table.

Relationship when Apart: This can be tough for both parties. The one at home may feel left behind and be resentful you are seeing great things or jealous of you meeting new people. If you are the one traveling, your heart and mind can be distracted by home, and you may feel resentful of being held back. Of course, these are extremes; if you are meant to be, you are meant to be. It is a big commitment staying together whilst apart, so it is very important to stay in contact, whether it be by mobile/text or Skype. Issues can be magnified when you are apart, so communicate. A text can so easily be misinterpreted, for example, so get on Skype and see each other face to face, cyber style! Of course, Skype is no substitute for seeing each other, so if you are going to be absent from each other for a prolonged period of time, schedule in a visit. Then you will both have something to look forwards to.

Organised Tour: This can be a relatively expensive way to travel compared to making arrangements independently. The itinerary is normally fixed (with optional extras) and rarely allows more than two nights in the same destination, leaving scarce spare time and the feeling you're being hurried. It can suit, however, the "cash rich, time poor" worker who doesn't have much time to plan or take off work. You are expected to eat all meals together, so the issue of claustrophobia can arise. This book concerns itself mainly with independent backpacking.

By now, you should have made up your mind to set off on your own or with someone else. Traveling as a group can be fun, but if there are more than two of you, you may develop different agendas on the road. It's harder to make collective decisions on where to eat, where to go, etc. The same advice above for pairs applies for traveling in a group: know your companions well enough that you can separate for a few days if you need some space. We'll continue on to planning.

Research and Trip Planning – Choosing Your Locations

With the internet, this bit has never been easier. You don't need to buy vast numbers of guidebooks, only never to use them. Start by making a list of countries you have dreamt of. Then look at a website such as Lonely Planet or Rough Guide and look at the "When to Go" or "Weather" sections for your dream countries. The "When to Go" advice may be influenced by the dry versus wet seasons, for example. Dry will generally be preferable but may prove more expensive since it usually means peak travel rates. The wet season can be fine if it means daily showers, but you'll want to avoid monsoons! In vast countries such as India, there may even be marked climactic differences between regions at the same time of year. Mark an approximate ideal visiting time next to each country you may want to see. Remember, spring in the northern hemisphere is autumn in the southern hemisphere and vice versa, so normally better to write the name of a month than a season. At this point, don't get bogged down in detail like how long are you expecting to spend in each.

How's it looking so far? You might have a list of between 8 and 20 destinations all with dates annotated next to them. When are you going away? Now write January through to December and box or circle the months you intend to travel. Put the countries against the respective months by best dates to travel. The "When to Go" section will normally list religious holidays and festivals – annotate these at the same time.

For example, if you intend on traveling from July through October and the following countries are on your list, this is an *extract* of how the list might look (please note caveat below box):

Jan	Cambodia			(Peru)				
Feb	Cambodia			(Peru)				
Mar		Jordan	Lebanon	(HK)		Japan	Mexico
Apr		Jordan	Lebanon	(HK)	SA	Japan	Mexico
May		Jordan	Lebanon		SA	Japan	(Mexico)
Jun				Peru	SA		(Mexico)
Jul	(Cambodia)	Ramadan	Ramadan	Peru		SA		(Mexico)
Aug	(Cambodia)	Ramadan	Ramadan	Peru		SA		(Mexico)
Sept	(Cambodia)	Jordan	Lebanon		(HK)	SA	Japan	(Mexico)
Oct	(Cambodia)	Jordan	Lebanon		HK	SA	Japan	Mexico
Nov	Cambodia	Jordan	Lebanon		HK	SA	Japan	Mexico
Dec	Cambodia			(Peru)	HK			
Notes	HK = Hong Kong; SA = South Africa Brackets indicate less preferable time either due to wet season with daily downpours or due to higher humidity than dry season Jordan/Lebanon – Ramadan in 2013 falls in July/August Peru – Jun/July/Aug best months for visiting Machu Picchu (Dec–Mar for beaches) SA – Jun – Sept best for hiking or wildlife spotting Japan – March/April = cherry blossom season Mexico – Nov 1st/2nd = Festival of the Dead							

As indicated above, you want to be semi-precise at this stage. Off-peak travel has its advantages – it is less busy, and prices for accommodation and airfares are lower. Nor does it rain all day during the low season in some countries, although you want to avoid countries where the wet season is a washout (in example above, May and June in Cambodia is monsoon season, but from July to October short downpours are more the norm, making those months second best to the dry season). Annotating your list for religious holidays helps, as, for example, Ramadan in Muslim countries may affect your travel plans. Annotating festivals also helps, whether you want to participate or to avoid them altogether (accommodation is scarcer and prices rise). If planning to include a festival, you'll need to be proactive in booking accommodation (see how to book under Accommodation later) to avoid paying much higher prices.

Now, look at the list again and have a think. What budget are you on? If you are on a shoestring budget, traveling in Japan will be off your radar, and North America or Australia can eat your budget away quite rapidly compared to Southeast Asia. But those regions are English-speaking and may suit the first-time traveler. Combining the two with a shorter time in the developed countries can be a good option. You can develop your confidence in traveling and finish in the cheaper regions, which may appear intimidating at first (indeed, many travelers do a well-trodden route of LA, Fiji, New Zealand, Australia and Southeast Asia, traveling from Singapore up to Bangkok and flying down to Cambodia, Laos, and Vietnam). Eliminate from your list one or two (e.g., Japan) at this point.

What timeframe do you have? Be realistic. Do you want to rush round a number of countries and get an impression of each (can be exhausting but has advantage that you can always go back to what you liked most!) or spend more time in one or two regions (and relax and submerge yourself in the culture)? How do you know how long to spend in each? How do you intend on getting to and from each country? If some on your list are adjacent, you might be able to go overland between them and reduce the number of flights you need. Are your routes and dates rigid or likely to be subject to change later? You might save money on a Round the World (RTW) ticket *beforehand* versus buying flights *ad hoc* once on the road, but there are restrictions with RTW tickets. At this juncture, it is worth digressing to describe a RTW ticket:

A RTW ticket is priced according to class of service, origin of travel, number of continents, mileage, and sometimes season. The traveler benefits from the optimized network of the airline alliance. However, these tickets are usually subject to restrictions. For example, the start and end of the journey almost always have to be located in the same country, and exactly one crossing *each* of the Atlantic and Pacific must be included in the itinerary. The number of stops is usually restricted to 3–16, and backtracking *between* continents (especially Europe and Asia) is usually restricted, although backtracking *within* a continent is usually permitted. The journey is normally pre-specified along with provisional dates (the outgoing flight has to be fixed). These dates may be changed en route at a local office of any airline in the alliance, but a change of destinations often results in an additional fee of up to USD150. If the next flight is left open-dated, the booking can be dropped by the airlines' computers.

Before you buy or browse the guidebooks of the countries you intend on traveling to, your next step is to call or visit a travel agent such as Flight Centre, STA, or Trailfinders. Their websites will have ready-made itineraries that may be more economical than your *wish list itinerary* but they can also offer tailor-made solutions. These travel agents are staffed by experienced travelers, who can help you whittle down your list and shape it to *almost* what you want (you may have to drop one or two destinations off the list due to ticket restrictions on backtracking, for example).

In our boxed example above, they would advise you that the following *would be possible* originating from London, for example: London - New York – Cancun (Mexico) – Lima (Peru) – Santiago (Chile) – Sydney (Australia) – Hong Kong – Tokyo (Japan) – Bangkok (Thailand) – make your own way to/back from Cambodia – Bangkok – Amman (Jordan) – London. You could also opt for some additional flights in Central or South America (to make up the maximum of 16 stops). However, *going overland reduces costs* (i.e, it is possible to travel between Peru and Chile). You would also have to exclude South Africa for two reasons. First, you cannot cross the Atlantic from London to USA and backtrack across the Atlantic from South America to South Africa. Instead, you have to continue in one direction and cross the Pacific, hence onwards to Sydney, before you hit your wish list in Asia. Second, if you did go in one direction, including South Africa on the itinerary between Bangkok and London would significantly increase the price. So before you've even traveled, you've learnt your first lesson in traveling – be flexible! You can always do South Africa as a discreet holiday, but you've gained the Sydney opera house and the floating markets of Bangkok as a bonus. That's not too bad, and you saved yourself buying the South Africa guidebook unnecessarily!

You've now spoken to a travel agent, whittled down your countries into an itinerary and discovered that your newly shaped route is *feasible*. You've also been given a heads-up on pricing of your ticket. *Don't buy your ticket now. You need to do a bit of reading first.* You can save yourself some money here by buying consolidated guidebooks by continent (e.g., Southeast Asia, Central or South America). You'll lose *only some* of the detail that individual country guidebooks will give you, but weight has to be your key consideration when selecting guidebooks! (see Books as a Type of Currency later for advice on how to buy or download and carry guidebooks). I'll now go onto budgeting – this will help you also decide how long to spend in each country or region. At this point, you should also be considering making an appointment to visit your doctor and/or travel clinic (see Vaccinations, Antimalarials and Health on the Road below).

Budgeting and Ticket Purchase

So you've almost decided your countries and route. How much money you actually needs depends on how you intend on getting round, what level of comfort you prefer, how you choose to eat and shop, and what sort of activities you intend on doing. You don't need to look at every single destination at this point. If, for example, you plan on going to eight countries, to stay in budget accommodation but eat out most of the time, and to travel by bus, take the most expensive destination in the guidebooks of the eight countries (usually the capital city), and jot down the average price of budget accommodation, the average price of a mid-range restaurant, and the price of a long-distance bus journey. Add them up and then add 20–25 per cent (you can be sure prices will have risen since the guidebook has been published). By using the most expensive city as a baseline and planning on eating out and getting transport every day, you will make sure to have more than enough. Street snacks, museum entrances, and occasional bus journeys will be more the norm for daily spending, so you have already factored in spare cash by budgeting higher per day than you'll actually spend (of course, there is the credit card for something you'd really regret not doing). Speaking from experience, it is better to go for a shorter time than to stretch out the time and live on the tightest of budgets. It can be nice to treat yourself with a cold beer after a long hike or the occasional splurge in a high-end restaurant.

Continuing our boxed example, if you're on a tight budget, accommodation and rail prices in and from Tokyo might cause you to drop it from your itinerary. By knowing how much money you have at your disposal and roughly how much your destinations will cost, you can *estimate* how long is ideal in each place. You don't want to be cutting your trip short or asking for money from home. If you have a rough idea of the costs ahead *and* you buy a RTW ticket that permits date changes, you'll also avoid the cost of route changes.

Make a separate budget for pre-trip expenses, which include the costs of vaccinations and visas (if any) as well as the purchase of hiking shoes, jacket, and the likes from an outdoor clothing company. Friends and family contributions are most welcomed here, as the pre-trip costs are not unsubstantial (see What to Bring below).

A percentage of you reading this might think, "Why not just purchase a set itinerary?" Well, a small bit of research effort at the beginning makes life enjoyable. Missing out on a major festival by days or not being able to hike a mountain range as the season has ended can be quite disappointing once you're there. It's worth talking to people who've already been to destinations, too, but remember: one person's opinion will not necessarily be yours. Listen to the reasons why someone has a negative opinion of a country. You'll sometimes hear people saying that "Brazil sucks" or "Peru sucks," etc. but it may be because they found Brazil was expensive and many hours were consumed on buses, or the Machu Picchu trail was closed or overbooked. In other words, they didn't do their homework beforehand!

You'll never be able to book a RTW trip that is *perfect* climatically or inclusive of all festivals. However, using our boxed example again, you might not make the Festival of the Dead in Mexico, but you'll avoid traveling during Ramadan. It may also be hot in July in New York, but you'll save money on purchasing equipment (e.g., a hiking jacket or shoes) you need there if you're organised. Importantly, however, the weather in our illustrated example should be conducive to uninterrupted travel across all the countries. The exampled itinerary allows you to see Mayan temples in Mexico, to hike to Machu Picchu, and to see Angkor Wat (Cambodia) and Petra (Jordan), amongst others.

If you've done your research and maths properly, perhaps you may have worked out that you could still have included Japan, for example, if you compromised on just visiting Tokyo. You've also probably worked out roughly how long you should spend in each place – remember, a RTW ticket is usually flexible on dates without penalty, so you can speed up a flight if you're not doing too well budget-wise on the road. *The key aim is to avoid being bailed out from home.*

You should now have worked out your route. There's just one thing to do before you contact the travel agent again - you should quickly check a website such as the Foreign and Commonwealth Office (FCO) or travel.state.gov (the US Department of State) for individual country advice. These websites are constantly updated with news of security situations or natural disasters, so they should be checked periodically as you travel.

You're now ready for your ticket purchase. Go back to the travel agent, repeat the itinerary, and get a reservation code for your trip, which they'll normally hold for 24 hours. Double check with a competing travel agent, and if the price cannot be matched, pay with your credit card (see Insurance and Money below). Whether through the same travel agent, another one, or online, you should purchase insurance simultaneously.

As a final note, RTW tickets can save you money versus ad-hoc ticket purchases, but jetlag is not to be underestimated. As advised in the Health section, taking it easy the first few days after crossing many time zones (e.g., Santiago to Sydney in our illustrated example) is advisable.

Insurance

You should *take out an insurance policy simultaneously to booking your ticket.* This means you'll have some cover if you have to postpone or cancel your trip for reasons such as ill health. If you pay with your credit card, you can claim a refund from the card company if the travel company goes bust. The policy should also be flexible enough so that you can extend the period of your cover if you decide to prolong your trip whilst traveling. If you'll be doing "extreme sports," you may need additional cover. Valuable items (such as camera equipment or laptop) will be subject to a limit. Some policies will include an excess on a claim, meaning you'll have to pay the first £50–100 on an individual claim. The price of an overall policy will depend on destinations, length of trip, age, whether you have pre-existing illnesses, and other variables, as well as any separate covers (e.g., for extreme sports). *Going for a cheap policy may actually be a "false economy"* – saving £50, for example, on the initial purchase may be offset if you have later to make a claim with a policy with a high claims excess (£100). There are a myriad of places to take out insurance policies from banks, the post office, supermarkets, and travel agencies to online. Indeed, online engines allow you to compare a multitude of policies simultaneously and to get free quotes. They can often be much cheaper due to lack of overheads and many have special deals and discounts for online policies only. The disadvantage of shopping online, however, is that you may not get clarification of policy terms, and you cannot ask advice. It may be a good idea therefore to first get some advice from the "high street" and then go online, compare various policies, and purchase one that has the best trade-off between price and cover. Always check the small print first. Regardless of what level of cover and policy you choose, they should have a 24-hour phone line and include the following:

Cancellation & curtailment cover: There are many reasons why a planned trip may have to be cancelled or delayed, whether due to your fault, that of one of the firms coordinating your travel, or entirely unforeseen circumstances. This cover may gain you compensation for a trip that had to be missed or cut short. Reasons for delay may include bad weather, natural disasters, unannounced strikes, or lost/stolen documents en route. A policy may cover the cost of extra accommodation or food needed as a result of the delay. Each policy has a daily maximum for reimbursement, and most will also have a set period of time that the trip must be delayed by before you can claim under the delay clause. Cancellation cover will also cover you for a flood or fire at your house, an accident en route, jury service, or sickness or injury to one of the party members. You won't, however, be covered for a change of plans or change of financial circumstances.

Legal expenses cover: This cover will account for a set sum towards any legal costs incurred from death, illness, or injury caused by a third party during your trip abroad. Policies will not provide cover for legal expenses that are against the insurance provider itself or a travel operator/agent. Under personal liability cover, some policies may pay you up to a set limit if you are found to be legally liable for accidental loss of or damage to someone else's possessions or accidental damage to another person. This will be invalidated if the damage arose from a criminal or malicious act on your part or the person is an employee or family member.

Baggage and personal belongings cover: Although this cover is "standard," the variation in cover between policies can be immense. Whilst most policies will compensate well for lost or delayed baggage, they may be more limiting when claiming for cash or personal belongings. Most policies cover only the value of an item when it was lost or stolen, not the cost of purchasing a replacement. The cover will be invalidated under carelessness (e.g., if you didn't take action to secure your possessions, such as lock your hostel door or window). All losses or thefts must be reported to the local police, and you must get an official report. Not having a report may impair your claim. With cash, you will be covered up to a certain value (see advice under Money section). Most policies will have a restrictive upper limit on a single item. You may be able to get additional cover on your household contents insurance for valuable items such as a laptop or digital camera, but there is normally a time limit on taking them abroad, so this may not work for long trips. You therefore have to weigh up the risk of loss and value versus merit of convenience. The loss of travel documents such as your passport is normally covered, and most policies will compensate a sum towards extra accommodation required whilst you seek a replacement. You should report the loss immediately to the local authorities and obtain a certificate of loss. As per the Documentation section, having your identification backed up will help speed up the replacement when visiting your nearest consulate.

Medical expenses cover: It may be distressing to lose money on a lost or stolen item, but medical cover is arguably the most important element of any travel insurance policy. An emergency abroad can be extremely expensive. If you need to be repatriated to your home country, it could cost you a fortune unless you are adequately insured. For example, the FCO website indicates that an air ambulance from the east coast of USA back to the UK can be up to £45,000 (and that is before any surgery costs, if any!). You and not your embassy or consulate will be liable for the cost. Emergency medical treatment or surgery (including dental sometimes) and the cost of returning your ashes home or holding a funeral where you die will normally be covered. Each policy will offer different levels of cover, but they will not pay for extra accommodation and travel expenses unless they has been deemed medically necessary.

Some countries will have reciprocal healthcare with your home country, which will lower the cost of your policy. When traveling to countries that don't have reciprocity, you need to ensure you have comprehensive medical cover. Wherever you are traveling, it is wise to ensure you are adequately covered.

Some events are never covered by travel insurance policies. These include self-inflicted injuries, interruption to a trip due to business or contractual commitments and war (some policies may cover for terrorism, however). With respect to the latter, it is important to check the advice given by the FCO both for your own personal safety and also because some insurance companies will not cover you for areas that are considered unsafe for travel.

As per the introduction, the cost of your policy is affected by the areas you choose to travel to and the length of your trip. Beware the insurance terminology. A "worldwide" policy will normally exclude USA & Canada (if you choose to include them, the price will increase). An "annual" policy can also be confusing – if you are planning a trip of a year, you'll want a *long stay* or *backpacker policy*, which is cover specifically aimed at anyone who will be traveling for long periods (typically up to 12 months, but choose one that is flexible and can be extended) and visiting a number of different countries in the same trip. "Annual" is *multi-trip* insurance, covering customers for an *unlimited number of trips within a year*, providing that each trip falls within the time limit specified by the insurance provider (typically 31 days but can be up to 60). Conversely, "single" trip cover will cover you *only for that trip* but can cover you for a specified time limit for up to 180 days (typically less)! This is why single-trip insurance is recommended for infrequent travelers. If you travel more than three times per year, it will usually be cheaper to purchase an annual multi-trip policy. To reiterate, ask the "high street" for advice, check the small print, and get the best trade-off between price and cover. You don't want to come undone later by a claim's excess or from cover exclusion.

Finally, as per the Documentation section, make sure you keep a record of your policy and note the numbers to call in your diary or email address book. If you need to buy a replacement of anything that is lost or stolen, keep the receipts safe. There is normally a specified time limit in which to make a claim upon return home, so be prompt. You will need to submit any receipts, including those for medical treatment or hotel stays, along with the police report or certificate of loss if applicable.

Section 2

Vaccinations, Antimalarials and Health on the Road

Make sure you visit your doctor and travel clinic as long as possible before going abroad (at least a month in advance). Discuss your destinations and find out what jabs and antimalarials you'll need and any additional health precautions you should take whilst there. If you're on prescribed medication, you may need to make arrangements to buy this privately. It is also important that you are both physically and mentally fit. You have to go with the right attitude.

Vaccinations

The vaccinations you'll need for the trip vary according to your destinations, how you intend on traveling (e.g., if you're not going to be amongst rice paddies, you won't be at risk for Japanese encephalitis), and how far in the past you've received doses already. For vaccinations, it helps getting a "health passport." That is simply a booklet that records what jabs you've had and when in one place – for example, a tetanus jab lasts ten years, so you won't need it again if your passport says you had one two years ago. Some travel vaccinations are free on your healthcare service (e.g., in the UK, currently these are the tetanus, diphtheria and polio booster, typhoid, hepatitis A and cholera, whereas others, such as hepatitis B, rabies, yellow fever, tuberculosis, and encephalitis must be paid for, regardless of whether you have the vaccinations at your doctor's or at a private travel clinic). If you're advised to have encephalitis or rabies jabs, you'll need two and three, respectively, with intervals of at least a week apart between each jab. A course of *either* can be as much as £150, so you'll need to factor this into your pre-trip budget (which should also factor in costs of any visas, if needed).

Antimalarials

If you are traveling to an area with a risk of malaria, your doctor will recommend you take antimalarial tablets. What you are prescribed will be based on the following factors: where you are going, your medical history, your current medications, any problems you have had with antimalarial medicines in the past, and whether you are pregnant. For example, of the different types of antimalarials, Lariam may not be appropriate for people who have had a history of mental illness such as depression. Each type is taken differently (daily or weekly) when in a malarial zone and for a differing time period before and after entering it (e.g., with Malarone, you'll commence taking the tablets two days before and finish the course seven days after exiting, but with Lariam, this will be three weeks before and four weeks after). The cost will vary by type of prescribed antimalarial and length of trip. If you are planning to go away for an extended period (six months or more) and you are traveling to different regions, you may only need to take antimalarials for part of your trip or require different antimalarials for different regions. Therefore, discuss your options at a specialist travel health clinic or your doctor's surgery as soon as possible.

Health

Prescribed Medication and Dental Check-Up

Make sure you have adequate supplies of any prescribed medicines that you normally take and pack them in your hand luggage. Check with the embassy of the country you are going to that your medication will be legal in that country. Inhalers and other common prescriptions and over-the-counter ("OTC") medicines are banned in some countries. Ensure your medication is in its original packaging, and carry a letter from your doctor with your full name, date of birth, and home address (that matches your passport) that describes briefly the nature of your illness, gives the generic and branded names of your medication, and says why you need to be carrying it. If you are on a long trip and the medication you'll need is bulky, you'll need to make arrangements for it to be sent (check import restrictions with the embassy or country's customs website), so find out the procedures in advance.

If your eyes haven't recently been tested, get another test and take a copy of your prescription (see Documentation). If you normally visit a dental hygienist every six months, also have a check-up before you leave.

Different countries have different policies towards dispensing the pill - some may sell it OTC (not all brands are available, though), whereas others may require you to see a doctor. Ensure you take a supply with you, therefore (most UK doctors will prescribe up to six months). Yeast infections commonly occur in hot climates or from being run down. If traveling with a partner, also use condoms. Whilst away, sanitary towels are available in most countries, as are tampons (sometimes behind the counter and not on display), but applicators are harder to find.

Health on the Road

Food and Drink

Travelers often get stomach upsets (and have stories to match!) due in large part to dirty food or water or to poor food hygiene and preparation. In developing countries, it's not unusual to see slabs of ice being transported on the back of a motorbike or fly-ridden meat hanging outside. If the tap water is unsafe to drink, use bottled water (check the seal isn't broken and use also when rinsing your toothbrush) and avoid products that likely contain tap water, such as ice cubes, ice creams, and salads. Ensure any meat or fish is cooked through, especially when eating street food. Diarrhoea can also be caused by change of diet, too much fruit, excessive alcohol consumption and overexposure to the sun.

Sun and Sea

If you've historically had only short periods of exposure to the sun, ease your way in as you'll have plenty of time to get a tan. There's nothing more painful (and embarrassing!) than excessive sunburn – it itches and is sore to the touch, making sleeping and wearing some types of clothing virtually impossible. Wear high sun factor, drink plenty of water to avoid dehydration (especially if consuming alcohol), and avoid the hottest parts of the day (11 am to 3 pm) by staying in the shade. If you are on your own and don't have someone to check on you periodically, look in the mirror when leaving the beach and going to the bathroom (take your valuables with you!) to see if you are burning.

Equally, if you're used to a swimming pool, the temptation to wade into the sea straight away will be big. If there's no lifeguard, check with a local first whether it's safe from riptides or jellyfish, for example, and don't dive in without checking the depth first (unfortunately paralysis has occurred when people have plunged into shallow water). Avoid swimming under the influence of alcohol and when alone in the dark (especially if female).

Alcohol and Drugs

Different countries have differing attitudes towards alcohol, so be aware of the culture and try not to offend. Drugs are generally illegal in most countries (although there are some exceptions by country and class of drug). Don't fall on the wrong side of the law. Recognise your limits (drinks overseas can be more alcohol and less mixer) and make sure that you are taking care of yourself - accidents and injuries are more likely to happen after drinking alcohol or taking drugs. If this happens, your travel insurance will likely be invalidated so you may be responsible for the cost of your hospital treatment abroad or repatriation home. As with your home country, never drive after drinking or taking drugs or get in a car with someone who has.

Sexual Health

If you'll likely be having sex, always carry and use condoms. This applies also to women: don't be persuaded by someone who doesn't want to use one, and come prepared yourself. Pack a supply before you go as they are not always readily available and can differ in quality (look for the British Standard Kitemark or European CE mark, indicating that the manufacturing was strictly controlled). Check the expiry date on the condoms and throw away any that are too old.

First Aid Kit

A lot of first-time backpackers go overboard on purchasing a ready-made first aid kit full of scissors, needles and antibiotics. Aside from the expense, in my experience such a kit takes up a lot of weight and is rarely used, and there's hardly anything you can't buy OTC. Better to put in your toilet bag or separate small medical bag some rehydration sachets such as Dioralyte (after bouts of diarrhoea), a few plasters, some blister covers (Compeed is a good brand) for after hiking, Savlon antiseptic for cuts, and Calamine lotion for sunburn, rashes, and insect bites or stings. Some sleeping aids (no prescription needed) such as Nytol can be useful also for bus journeys and dorm rooms. You could also place here mosquito repellent, but local alternatives (coils, soaps and sprays) also exist in most countries.

However cautious you may be on the road, accidents can happen. To reiterate, make sure you have adequate insurance cover, which needs to cover you for medical and repatriation costs as well as any dangerous sports or activities you may be undertaking.

Passports and Visas

Passports

Make sure the expiry date on your passport is *at least* six months beyond the length of your trip, in line with some country entry requirements but also giving you flexibility to extend your trip. Some immigration authorities are "stamp happy" – have enough blank pages to allow for visas and entry/exit stamps. If you need a new one, check with your government's passport website how quickly you can get a replacement. For example, in the UK you can get a one week or same-day replacement for a premium if you really need to, but you should normally apply at least four weeks before your trip. However, if you are applying for your first passport, you may have to apply at least six weeks beforehand. In most cases, the passport office will require that you attend an interview. It goes without saying that you shouldn't book and pay for your trip until your passport application has been accepted.

Visas

Once you know what countries you intend on visiting, check with the consulates or embassies you intend on traveling to (look at their websites, as requirements may have changed since your guidebook was published) to see whether you require a visa. Alternatively, many travel agents, such as Trailfinders, will give this information for free. You can queue in person at an embassy, apply by post (always use recorded delivery), or use a visa service such as Trailfinders for an extra fee, which is quicker and may save you taking a day off work. You'll normally need to include passport photos in your application. Most visas are valid for use within three months of issue. On long trips, therefore, it may not be practical to obtain one prior to your trip, as it will expire before you arrive in that country. Many countries will issue them on arrival for often a smaller fee than obtaining it in your home country (bring passport photos again!) but may only give you a single-entry and not multiple-entry visa. In this case, if you are planning on traveling to an adjacent country overland and returning to the original country, you will have to apply and pay for a second single-entry visa to re-enter. You will therefore have to factor in this additional cost. Be patient when applying at a border; showing anger or frustration will not help your application. Never try and bribe your way in – you're dealing with foreign laws and foreign language so could land yourself in trouble with the authorities. The general message is, again, be early with your planning: add an extra two to three weeks to the passport timeframe if you need a visa or two.

Final Preparations

This is the least fun and most stressful part. There are a volume of small tasks to tend to before leaving for a long trip other than just arranging a farewell party. If you're a school leaver, it might be easy; otherwise, things you may have to do include:

- Sub-letting your room; or
- Approaching an estate agent to market your property for rent, accepting tenancy references, arranging an inventory check and the transfer of utility bills. You may need some work done to your property prior to marketing it, and you'll need to be financially organised before, during, and after your trip so as to file your tax return later (keep all receipts);
- Taking out landlord's insurance;
- If there are contracts such as alarms or ground rent that need to be paid whilst away, switch to direct debit if you're used to responding by post;
- Putting your belongings into a storage facility;
- Arranging the redirection of your post to someone willing to accept it.

The final stage is Documentation whilst you do your shopping (see What to Bring, How to Pack and How to Carry It) before organising your leaving drinks and then getting on your way!

Documentation

With the internet and email, the beauty is that you don't have to keep photocopies of all your documentation *in your bag* anymore, which leaves you open to identity fraud. But it will still be necessary to make photocopies. This process may seem like a hassle, but it doesn't take a lot of time and will save you an awful lot of effort if your passport is stolen or you need to make an insurance claim.

Start by photocopying the photo page of your passport. After you've scanned it, get it laminated. Then photocopy and scan your driving license and birth certificate (the three combined will greatly speed up the process of obtaining a temporary passport from an embassy abroad if your passport is lost or stolen). It is a grey area whether *color* photocopying your passport is legal or not, so to be safe, you can photocopy in black and white. The UK's Identity and Passport Service (IPS) does not recommend copies, as carelessness of retention can lead to identity fraud.

Scan your flight itinerary (if you booked a RTW ticket) and travel insurance details. Also scan copies of your traveler's cheques and receipt if you've decided to use them (see Money below).

Staple your receipts for large purchases (a backpack, waterproof jacket, etc.) to an A4 piece of paper, and then photocopy and scan it. This documentation will be useful if you have to make an insurance claim.

If you've rented out your house, scan a copy of your lease and your landlord insurance. Scan, too, a copy of the contents list of your storage facility, if you used one.

If you wear glasses, make a copy of your prescription in case of need of replacement. If you are on prescribed medication, scan a copy of the letter from your doctor. Scan your yellow fever certificate if you needed one (see Vaccinations), but do in these instance take the originals with you.

Store all these scanned documents in your email account so you can have easy instant access to them if later need be. As described in the Preserving Memories/Electrical Equipment section, if you're using a public PC to print these off later, remember to unclick "keep me signed in" or "remember password"; clear the downloads after – you don't want the next user to have access to your details.

Section 3

What to Bring, How to Pack and How to Carry It

Before we get onto the selection of what to bring and how to pack, it is worth saying now that your backpack will be your "mobile home" – you'll be living out of your new wardrobe for the duration of your trip. Many first-timers will make the mistake of taking too much and throwing stuff away as it is either a) too heavy or b) seldom used. Indeed, even if you pack lots of stuff, you'll find you only use a fraction of it anyway, as you'll develop a favourite t-shirt for hiking or a favourite pair of shorts for lounging in. After the end of a long trip, even the most materialistic of people will discover that you don't really need that much. Many friends or family members prior to your trip may want to give you something material to take away. But it's not them who will be carrying it for months on end! It's far more useful if they gave you cash or gift vouchers for an outdoor clothing company (for the stuff you actually need!) or a travel clinic. So practice saying it now: "No thanks Grandma, I'd rather have the cash!"

What you ought to take will depend on the length of trip, whether you'll be in cold (including high-altitude) or warm climates, where you intend on staying, and what kind of activities you'll do. This section will cover the vast majority of people – that is, those that stay in hostels day-to-day. Unless you are the most meticulous planner (e.g., you make your final destination a cold climate and either buy a jacket then or get someone to post it to you at your final destination) or plan your trip around just one type of travel (hot climates only, for example), it is hard to avoid the need to carry a mixture of both warm and cold clothing. This usually means a quarter of your backpack (in terms of space) is filled with things you rarely use. Therefore it's important that you carry lightweight stuff such as a nylon or polyester shell rain or windproof jacket. As a general rule, though, never carry anything you're worried about losing! Before going on to what to bring, let's start with the most useful items on your pre-trip shopping list, the backpack and daysack.

Backpack

I would go for one that has two sets of zips and can be padlocked from the top and bottom (you want to be able to access your things from top and bottom). Ones that unclip from the top and have a drawstring leave you vulnerable to theft in dorm rooms or luggage rooms. Ones with side pockets look tempting, but they are rarely padlockable. It is better to use a "cube" (see below) for those items you want easy regular access to. Backpacks generally go up to 95L. If you go for a bigger size one, you don't have to pack it to the brim. You'll want to pick things up from time-to-time and send them home so leave some space. Karrimor is one brand that makes backpacks that are expandable/collapsible by up to 20L (e.g., 70–90L). This is perfect for the flexibility of carrying extra in the *same bag* when you need to but minimising weight at other times by collapsing it to the right size. You'll also want adjustable shoulder straps to take the pressure off your back. The backpack should preferably be of waterproof construction or have built-in waterproof covers that unzip and fold over the front. Many have a compartment with a cover that unrolls and secures the straps – this is quite handy for airports, as it stops them getting caught in conveyor belts, etc.

Practicality is the key. When purchasing, try it on and ask the sales assistant to help you adjust the straps. Image is irrelevant – avoid one with bright colours (stands out to a thief) or kick some dust into it once purchased so it doesn't look brand new. There are gender differences when purchasing a backpack – men will need a larger backpack, not because they can carry more but because their clothes are generally bulkier (e.g., trousers are heavier and more voluminous than skirts) and their shoes will take up more room.

Daysack

Many backpacks come with a small (on average 10L) zip-off daypack. In practical terms, they're not very useful. They are too small when full with items such as guidebook, camera, sunglasses and water, and you won't be securing it to the backpack anyway (they should be carried on your front or over the shoulder with combination lock). If the backpack is right, leave behind the small "freebie" and buy a separate slightly larger daysack. It should be durable (i.e., the straps won't strain if loaded) but not so large that it won't fit in a hostel locker.

What to Bring

The following list doesn't look like much, but there are cheap laundry services in most destinations. And contrary to at home, you'll be amongst the league of unwashed and won't be changing your clothing every day! The first checklist concerns clothing and is not definitive but *indicative* of what you should contemplate:

Essentials	Other Clothing
Warm jacket (not high street fashion brand but from outdoor clothing shop)	Underwear/socks (double layered socks useful if running/hiking)
Lightweight rain jacket	2 pairs of shorts
Pyjamas (for dorm use)	3 t-shirts (women can substitute for vests, but you'll need at least 1 t-shirt as shoulders need to be covered when visiting temples and in Muslim countries)
Combat trousers (with secure side pockets)	1 lightweight pair of trousers (or 2 lightweight dresses)
Hiking shoes/trainers	2 long-sleeved tops (including shirts)
Flip flops/sandals	1 thin jumper
Swimming attire (trunks/bikinis – 2 maximum)	1 pair of jeans (optional due to weight/volume)
	1 polyester running top (optional but lightweight and soaks up sweat so great for hiking)

The following box lists the other items you should consider. "Luxuries" are those items that aren't strictly necessary but may make your trip more comfortable or enjoyable.

Essentials	Luxuries
Head torch (better than handheld torch, as there'll be times you want both your hands free)	Mask & snorkel – for the avid diver but will also save you money not having to rent each time you want to snorkel
Travel towel (compact and dries quickly)	Waterproof camera case (e.g., by Aquapac – great for basic underwater pictures)
Sarong (serves as an additional towel or a sheet and is useful on beaches)	Plastic playing cards – don't get wet and rip so excellent for drinking games

Chain (for securing backpack – see Safety/Accommodation)	
Basic medical kit (see Health section)	
Plastic zip wallet (for documents)	ELECTRICALS – see Preserving Memories/Electrical Equipment below
Multi-adaptor	
Toilet bag (should be zippable and placed inside a plastic bag, as they can be crushed and leak fluids)	

A quick perusal of your guidebook might also suggest a sleeping bag and mosquito net, but these are rarely used, take up space, have an upfront cost, and can very often be hired (if not freely available). Other items that are "nice haves" such as a penknife also have upfront costs, are rarely used, and could be substituted for nail scissors in your toilet bag, for example. People very often get carried away by packing what they might need, such as a sewing kit – the reality is that a tailor is never far away and will stitch up a rip for only a few dollars. The general message, therefore, is not to go buying expensive "once in a while" items. Pack the light and necessary, and don't carry anything you're worried about getting lost or stolen (sentimental or value-wise). Your insurance policy will have a limit on individual items.

How to Pack and How to Carry It

To reiterate, don't pack too much at the outset, as there'll be stuff you'll want to pick up en route. Generally speaking, you're best off to keep the heavy weight (e.g., hiking boots) slightly lower in the backpack for better balance by keeping the weight near your centre of gravity and close to your back. Balancing the weight between left and right is also vital. If you get the weight distribution correct, your backpack will feel more like it is a part of your body than just dead weight on your back.

Within the backpack, there are a few things that are useful to have. Bin liners are useful for separating dirty laundry or wet bathing items from clean, dry clothing. Some people (or fashionistas!) use compression sacks, which compress clothes down to a fraction of their size. It is better, in my opinion, to carry less; appearance generally doesn't matter for a traveler. Packing "cubes" or organisers can be great, however, to organise your clothes or gear in your pack by either separating things you rarely use so they're out the way when rummaging through your bag *or* consolidating the things you want easy access to. They are inexpensive, are made from lightweight nylon mesh with an easy-view window, and have a zip.

Roll your clothes when packing your backpack to create more room. Leave the heavier or more voluminous items that you'll use infrequently (e.g., jeans) at the bottom and the lighter items you use more regularly (e.g., underwear, t-shirts) at the top. If you're packing a backpack for the first time, you'll find you've probably filled it to the brim because of not rolling your clothes and packing two more t-shirts and an additional pair of shorts. About 10–20 per cent of your backpack should remain free. When moving around town and especially transport terminals, wear your daysack on your front and not on your shoulders.

Money

So you've done the budgeting and you're wondering how you access your money and how to carry it. Leave plenty of time to sort this out; there are quite a few things you need to consider before you leave for abroad. These are listed under the different methods of payment.

Generally speaking, ATMs will be the main source of cash, so you'll need at least one debit card. A credit card can be used for emergencies (such as medical bills) or splurge activities *but* can also be used for cash withdrawals from an ATM with your pin number if your debit card is lost, damaged, or stolen. Having at least one debit and credit card is advisable. However, paying by debit or credit card in some countries leaves you vulnerable to fraud (e.g., card cloning), so it always pays to have cash on you. You can also obtain local currency by exchanging traditional traveler's cheques, but this relies on banks and foreign exchange locations being open. A newer phenomenon is a reloadable prepaid card called a "cash passport" and offered by Travelex.

ATMs

ATMs are either external to a building and open 24 hours or available inside a bank or shop during opening hours. Where there is an ATM both inside and outside the bank and it is during opening hours, it is better in some countries to use the one inside. This makes you less visible to a potential tailgating bystander. Try not to take money out at night except in well-lit, public places, and never let anyone get too close when making a withdrawal.

> Tip: In some countries (e.g., Argentina), the cash is dispensed before the card is ejected. This in most cases will be contrary to your home country, where the card is ejected and the cash is dispensed after. It may seem common sense, but don't walk off before you've ended the transaction and collected your card. Many a traveler I've met has had their card swallowed up by the machine! What to do if this happens? If it is during bank hours, contact the staff immediately, who should be able to recover your card; if it is after hours, cancel your card immediately by contacting your bank. This is one reason why it is better to use an ATM attached to a bank, as one located within a convenience store, for example, cannot be opened by the staff.

Debit and Credit Cards

The most commonly accepted cards in ATMs or in shops/restaurants are Visa and Mastercard for both debit and credit cards. The transaction fee on the credit card is usually higher than the debit card. If you have been receiving monthly paper statements, you should consider switching to online banking. If you are going to be using your credit card whilst away, you can set up an email alert when your monthly statement is ready. With online banking, wherever there is internet connectivity, you can access your accounts 24/7 to check your balance or make transactions (such as paying your credit card balance with your debit card). Alternatively, you can arrange with your bank for a friend or relative to become a signatory on your account to pay bills on your behalf, but this relies on them being organised and not away themselves. Better to take control of your own finances by selecting online banking.

If you use one of your cards to make payments, never let it leave your eyesight. The payment should be made in front of you or you run the risk of your card being cloned. Fees for a purchase may be higher than for a cash withdrawal. Of course, there are benefits from using a card, such as carrying less cash or receiving awards points for money spent. Many large transactions can also be done securely via online banking and PayPal. A debit card or credit card can also be used over the counter at a bank to withdraw cash. You'll need proof of ID, such as a passport.

Before you go:

1. Let the bank know in advance that you are going away and list the countries and approximate dates that you are going. Otherwise you may try to withdraw cash from an ATM only to find that your transaction is declined. This is because the banks put a stop on transactions they consider "suspicious." Even if

you have contacted your bank prior to your trip, they may put a stop on your card anyway; certain countries, such as Brazil, trigger an internal alert.

The reality is that you'll then have to find an internet cafe or phone booth (or wifi spot if using a laptop) and ring the customer services number on the back of the card, who will contact the fraud department to unblock your card. This process of reactivating your card may take time, and making the call itself will require cash. A credit card with pin number can be used, but this attracts a higher fee – that is, if they haven't put a temporary block on your card too! That is why I travel with two debit cards and two credit cards (a mixture of Visa, Mastercard, and Amex) and have a spare stash of cash (around USD25) separated from my valuables in case I cannot contact the bank during work hours and need to pay for a night's accommodation and phone call the following morning.

2. Check the expiry date on your debit or credit cards. If the expiry date is during your trip, contact the bank to reissue you a new card in advance of your trip.

3. You may also want to consider raising your daily limit on withdrawals. This will allow you more flexibility, e.g., to pay a larger transaction in cash rather than possibly incurring any applicable credit card fees.

Cash

In most countries, you pay in local currency. However, the Euro or US dollar (USD) is accepted in many developed and developing countries outside the Eurozone where the currency is unstable. In fact, in some countries such as Ecuador and El Salvador, the US dollar *is* the official currency. It pays to have a mixture of both local and major currencies. You might use USD for "large" expenditures, such as a white-water rafting expedition (which saves you carrying large numbers of local currency notes) and local currency for "small" expenses such as a local bus (you'll get a better exchange rate).

Before you go:

An ATM should be available at most destination airports, but they rarely dispense small denominations. Get from your bank or from a foreign exchange USD150–200 worth of USD and local currency in small denominations, as the taxi driver from the airport likely either won't have change or will pretend not to have change in order to get a forced tip. After that, always try to break a big note when possible and hold on to your small change. These notes will be useful both for tipping and for local buses or small shops. Please note that marked notes or ripped and sellotaped notes aren't always accepted. If given these as change, insist on a normal note.

> Tip: Check in your guidebook before you reach a destination whether an ATM is listed. It is annoying getting caught out and having to partially backtrack to get some cash. Don't always assume you can pay by card.

Traveler's Cheques

Traveler's cheques come in a variety of the major currencies (e.g., British Pound, USD, Euro and Japanese Yen) and denominations, can be used in many countries around the world, and can be refunded if lost or stolen. Of course, commission will be charged, which will vary by country and agent.

Before you go:

Record the serial numbers of your traveler's cheques in your email account and diary in case you need to call to replace them.

Travelex Cash Passport

Through Travelex, you obtain a prepaid currency card (available in seven major currencies) that is not linked to your bank account. You can top up your balance and check it online, and it can be used in merchants or ATMs

Wire Transfers

If you've run out of cash or need it in an emergency at short notice, it is possible to receive funds on the same day. Branches of wire transfer companies such as Western Union are in most countries and especially prevalent where family members work overseas and send cash back to their families. A friend or relative can send money online, by phone, or in person, and you can pick it up (minus the fee!) from a branch with proof of ID. If you've still got your cards, it is less expensive to get someone to send money to you via online banking. This option charges no fee but can take up to three business days, so the wire option is for those who need cash almost instantly.

Black Market

Changing money on the black market is quite common practice in countries where the official rate is less than the unofficial (e.g., Venezuela), so most travelers on a budget are tempted to acquire money by these means. Changing money this way is technically illegal (despite it being commonplace) and incurs risks both in terms of the authorities and being scammed. Be discreet, and try and change money in a hostel or shop rather than the street. You get a better exchange rate the more you change, but change only a small amount at first until you're familiar with the new currency. The moneychanger may try and give you forged notes or a defunct currency or use "magician's tricks" to withhold a few notes when counting the money out to you, so count it yourself. Be aware they may even use a rigged calculator - if you're bad at maths, use the calculator on your phone to sanity check it.

FX Rates – Know before You Buy!

Before you enter a country, go online and check the latest foreign exchange (FX) rates. A good website is www.oanda.com, whereby you can click on the Currency Converter link and check the FX rate versus your home country's. It's a good idea to check it against the USD as well since this is widely accepted and interchangeable. If maths is not your forte, write the exchange rate and some multiples of it on the inside of your guidebook or a piece of paper kept in your wallet/purse. For example: at the time of writing, £1 = 2.96 TRY (Turkish Lira); £3 would therefore be roughly 9 TRY. If you are shopping in a souk and haggling on price, if you've written it down like this, you should be able to calculate that the quoted price of 10 TRY would be roughly £3.5 and will appear more confident and competent. As a rule of thumb, a typical street vendor will quote a price two to three times the actual price at which they make a profit. As an example, they would be willing to sell an item at 30–50 per cent of an original quoted price. They will pretend they are offended by selling at that price and imply they are doing you a favour after declaring numerously it is "handmade, not machine" and "better quality, not same same," but all they have done is start with an inflated price. Don't show that you are too interested, as this will reduce your bargaining credibility, and feel free to use the "walk away" trick – that is, walk away when you are close to securing a deal. A merchant will often call you back and bring the price down a bit in response. This advice is valid in countries worldwide, but losing your temper arguing in Eastern Asia can be a cultural taboo. This advice should be ignored if the item was very little to begin with (i.e., less than £1: just pay up – it's their livelihood!). No-one likes to be ripped off; however, even if you don't think you're getting a "deal" in that country, think what you would pay for the same item in your home country before you decide to walk away permanently.

Discount Cards

A number of countries cater well for travelers and have discount cards and vouchers available for museum entrances, accommodation, and activities. However, if you are a full-time student, you can make a number of savings if you travel with an International Student Identity Card (ISIC). There is also the International Youth Travel Card (IYTC) for anyone aged under 26 and the International Teacher Identity Card (ITIC). Membership of the Youth Hostel Association (YHA) or Hostelling International (HI) Association can save you money on accommodation, products, and services, too.

As a final note, I consider books as a type of currency. In most hostels, restaurants, or cafes, once you've finished a book, you can exchange it for another for free. Bring two from home – if you've read one and not the other but you spot a better book, you can exchange the second one. But if you've only got one, you have to ditch your book, whether you've finished it or not. Normally, it is accepted to exchange a novel for a novel but not a novel for a guidebook; you can only exchange a guidebook for a guidebook if there are two of the type you want already there. Don't automatically assume you can pick up your guidebooks on route by this method, but equally, don't carry a year's worth of guidebooks with you. You can attempt to swap with travelers going in the other direction, although some like to keep their annotated guidebooks for sentimentality. Better, as part of your pre-trip planning, work out where on route you can reserve guidebooks or order them in advance. Failing that, you can download the whole guidebook or individual chapters from *Lonely Planet* or get someone from home to post them to you. Rather than exchange, there's also a fun website whereby you can give your book away (www.bookcrossing.com) - you register your book for free, download a label with assigned ID to stick on your book, and either give it to someone or leave it in a hostel or cafe. If the recipient registers the book ID from the label, you can track where in the world it is. Imagine leaving it in Hong Kong and seeing it in Holland.

How to Carry Your Money and Valuables

Try never to have your valuables visible. An external "bum bag" is not a good idea. Neither is concentrating your valuables all in one place. Leave some valuables in your bag back at the hostel (in a locker or chained and padlocked – see Safety/Accommodation) and some on your person (on your body or in a zippable daysack). A money belt can be concealed under your clothes, but in my experience, the strap at the back can ride up and the whole thing can stick to you uncomfortably in the heat. I carry both a wallet with one debit card, a laminated passport copy, and enough cash for that day and a business card holder (slim and barely noticeable in your pocket) with another debit or credit card in it. The third and fourth card should be securely kept in the hostel. If you're confronted by a robber, hand over the wallet. Don't be a hero; it's not worth losing your life for a day's budget! Besides, you're insured!

Carry your valuables inside zipped or buttoned pockets. In some countries, you'll often need your original passport to obtain bus tickets, for example. Have this in your concealed money belt (not a visible pocket!) or in your zipped-up daysack along with your camera and guidebook, and don't "advertise your wealth" by hanging it around your neck (see Personal Safety). However you decide to carry your money, never have more than a few days' worth of cash on you. As aforementioned, insurance companies will place a limit on lost or stolen cash that can be replaced.

Preserving Memories

You've taken time out from your life and have spent money on your trip, so you may as well preserve the memory! For some, this may take the form of a journal/diary (private) or for others a blog (public). Regardless of who you are, preserving photos and videos has never been easier with the advent of the internet. It means no more boxes of rolled film and negatives and no more bulky VHS cassettes. It can also be free or relatively inexpensive. For backing up your photos and videos, please see the Electrical Equipment section below.

A *journal* or *diary* can be more than just a cross-reference to your photographic dates and locations. As well as recording people you've met and places you've been to, you can make it more of a scrapbook with Pritt stick and scissors, sticking in anything from ticket stubs of museums/attractions to foreign beer labels. Someone you've traveled with can comment and sign it, and it can be fun to read the whole thing back years later. If you decide to do this, try to keep it updated regularly (every couple of days). You can quickly forget where you've been and what and whom you've seen, even when traveling with a companion!

> Tip: If you don't have a great memory, you can hide within your diary usernames for banking, but please disguise them in case of theft or loss. For example, if you have an account with Barclays with a login of HK258412, don't write "Barclays" in your diary (you know you have an account with them!) and change the login, for example, to JL369523, one key right on the keyboard in each case. This will be nonsensical to the recipient if it falls into their hands. Never write down your passwords. There will be a password reminder prompt such as first school, mother's maiden name, etc., or you can reset your password and change it back to something memorable. It's a good idea here also to note telephone numbers for lost or stolen cards, but you could also do this under your contact lists in your email account.

A *blog* is essentially an online picture diary of your trip. You can list your destinations and upload graphics (pictures and videos) and make commentary. The word blog is derived from weblog (web + log). By default, a blog is completely public and can be read by anyone on the internet, which can raise issues of copyright and intellectual property. However, a blog is interactive, allowing visitors to leave comments and messages, which can be fun or interesting for the blogger. You can elect, however, to keep it private by changing the settings so that just you or just your chosen readers can access your blog (which can be nice for close friends and family who don't have to wait until you're home to see your photos and hear your stories). Serious bloggers can in fact monetise their pages with click-throughs and advertisements.

> Tip: A blog requires internet access (not always available) and time/commitment. If you want a break from writing, this may not be for you. If you have an audience and commit to a fortnightly or monthly blog update, the novelty may soon transform to an obligation. I've met many a traveler who's used the words "I *have to* update my blog later" and missed out on the current happenings. A blog can always be written retrospectively if you use a diary/journal. If you're still unsure what they're about, have a look on sites such as blogtopsites.com to see what other people are doing. You can also blog privately to start and then change the settings to public later.

Electrical Equipment

With the advent of the internet, travel has never been easier. Sixteen years ago, there were no internet cafes or wifi, communication was via phone cards and faxes, mail was received via *poste restante* (a mail collection service offered by post offices) and there was no way of backing up your photos other than sending the rolled film home. However, the more electronics you take, the more you have to carry and protect from thieves or damage. I often say that a universal plug socket and charger would be far more valuable to travelers than a universal currency, given all the space adaptors and chargers take up. However, being on the road without music or not having a good camera are not something I would contemplate, and a small portable laptop is advantageous for photo uploading and making banking transactions online securely. What you take is up to you, but the following information is something for you to consider.

Photography

For some, one camera is sufficient, but I travel with two cameras. Why? I have one lightweight, slim camera that fits in my pocket and is perfect for nights out and one that I use for landscapes and scenery. Also, on long trips, inevitably something goes wrong with one of them. If your camera is new, it may be covered by warranty in your home country, but this involves sending it home, in which case you are camera-less for a couple of weeks and have no idea where you will be for it to be sent back to you once repaired. Common problems are water or sand within the lens. In countries such as Peru, it is perfectly possible to have someone take it apart with tweezers, clean it with a toothbrush, and put it back together within a few hours for very little money. In more technological countries such as Japan, surprisingly, broken cameras need to be sent to the manufacturer, which can take up to two weeks. Having two means you can go out at night without worrying about your "good" camera. You also have a better camera for those photos you want to impress the folks back home whilst having the peace of mind that comes with knowing you won't have to shell out for a new one as you travel if one goes wrong!

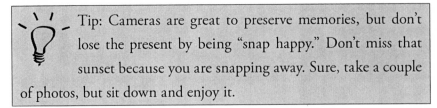

Tip: Cameras are great to preserve memories, but don't lose the present by being "snap happy." Don't miss that sunset because you are snapping away. Sure, take a couple of photos, but sit down and enjoy it.

Laptop

The question of whether to take a laptop along is difficult. On trips of a year or so, the money you spend on visiting internet cafes will be pretty much equal to the initial purchase cost of the laptop. On shorter trips, a laptop may not be necessary; you'll be back home before you know it, and a laptop is just another thing to worry about carrying. Many hostels, hotels, and cafes have wifi, as do airports and public areas (look for the wifi logo). If you have a laptop, you can upload your photos online (see section) whilst you eat in a restaurant or chat to other travelers in your hostel living room without locking yourself away in an internet cafe for a couple of hours being unsociable, hungry and thirsty, and vexed of the local music, as is often the case! Also, internet cafes do not always have the right antivirus software protection or eliminate search histories. Using your own laptop, you can ensure your online banking or transactions are more secure, and your photo card will be free from contracting a virus (see Card Reader below). Laptops needn't take up too much room, either. An HP Mini, for example, has the dimensions 6.6 x 10.3 x 0.95 inches, and an Acer is roughly similar. If you decide not to buy or take one, remember to always unclick "keep me signed in" or "remember password," as otherwise you may remain logged in when you think you have signed off, leaving you vulnerable to people accessing your accounts or social networking sites.

> Tip: Google "free wifi spots" plus country you are in. For example, if you are in the USA, type "free wifi spots USA" and you'll find www.wififreespot.com. For Europe and Japan, you'll find www.free-hotspot.com and www.freespot.com/users/map_e.html, respectively.

Multi-Adaptor and Multi-Plug

Available in most travel agencies or airports, a multi-adaptor is a single plug with clip-on chargers for the major brands of mobiles as well as iPods. Need to put that plug in the local socket? A multi-plug is available in major travel agencies and airports too. You simply put the multi-adaptor into the multi-plug, which has a variety of endings to fit all sockets worldwide. If you forget to buy one before you go, a local plug adaptor can often be bought in marketplaces. For example, in Latin America, look out for a sign that says "*ferreteria*" or a local vendor with cardboard boxes full of adaptor plugs.

Music

Smaller than the old Walkman/cassette players of bygone days, iPods or MP3 players take up very little room and are great for long bus journeys.

> Tip: Downloading some audiobooks before you go away can be great to listen to. If you will be traveling in a pair, a splitter is a great device that allows two people to listen to the same thing. Want other people to listen to it as well? Why not invest in speakers? It can be great fun to have a party in your room or on the deck of a boat or on the beach.

Card Reader

Available from electrical outlets or photo shops, this device plugs straight to a PC. You put your memory card in the card reader rather than directly in the PC, eliminating the possibility of a virus being contracted, which risks loss of your photos and redundancy of your memory card.

Phone/Skype

Skype is free to download on your laptop and is prevalent in most internet cafes so is great to make free calls to people. Most cafes will have a camera so the other person can see you (and be jealous of your tan!). Get your nearest and dearest to invest in a camera – you want to see them too! You can add Skype credit too for a better connection and phoning businesses that aren't in your Skype contacts. Skype definitely saves money, but for a better connection, many internet cafes have phone booths where you can phone home. They advertise the prices outside for ringing most countries and are differently priced for fixed landlines and mobiles.

Mobile

On longer trips, paying monthly fees for mobile phones can be expensive, so a pay-as-you-go option could be considered. To get the cost of the texts down, buy local SIM cards as you go round. There is no need for the extra charger if you have a multi-adaptor, and a pay-as-you-go phone is good for emergencies - even if you don't use it regularly, friends and family can text you if they need to contact you urgently. If you take a phone on monthly subscription, Viber is a free text message/calling system as long as you are connected to wifi.

External Hard Drive

Available in various storage sizes from generally 250GB to 1TB, you can drag photos or videos from your laptop onto this and store them. How much do you need? As an indication, over one year's worth of photos and videos will be close to 50GB if you're an avid photographer, so 250GB should be plenty, even if you put some films for viewing on your laptop on it in advance. On a short trip, you may consider storing photos online and backing them up when you are home if you are worried about your whole life being on the hard drive.

Uploading Photos

My experience of meeting people is that they always lose their photos in the last couple of weeks because they let their guard down and relax. My motto is "Back up, back up, and back up again" – that is, on the laptop, on an external hard drive, and on an online hard drive. Of course, you can just back up in an internet cafe using an online hard drive (e.g., Dropbox) but again, use a card reader device – they are cheap, and it stops you from possibly getting your camera memory card infected.

There are numerous websites dedicated to storage. Some are quicker for downloading photos and can be cheaper (the more you print, the cheaper it is) and save you time creating albums manually after a trip, but you will lose the original digital file resolution unless you pay for the per-image download or if they are not backed up elsewhere. For those who do not wish to edit the originals, this may not matter. In conclusion, therefore, digital photographs give you no negatives to fall back on so I would recommend adopting one or two online storage options, as your laptop or external hard drive may be stolen, corrupted, or damaged. With some websites even allowing you to crop and edit photos, choose what is right for you. Take the time before you travel to read the small print, look at the differences, and set up an account that works for you. After all, you've taken time out from your life and have spent money on your trip. You may as well preserve the memory!!

> Tip: On longer trips, you'll notice when uploading photos that you're wearing the same thing over and over again. Refresh your "wardrobe" every couple of months by chucking the odd t-shirt out and buying a cheap new one.

Vegetable & Fruit Stall, Bocas Del Toro (Panama)

Street Vendor, Valladolid (Mexico)

Loading Up the "Chicken Bus" (Guatemala)

"Chicken Buses", Xela (Guatemala)

"Chicken Bus" Vendors (Guatemala)

Inner City travel, near Perquin (El Salvador)

"Day of the Dead Festival", Oaxaca (Mexico)

Underway

Transport and Getting Around

So you've landed in your first country and met a few people. Now you want to travel onward. How do you get around? There are numerous methods of travel, all varying by price, speed, and safety. This section covers them by turn. If you are on a tight schedule and in a vast country (such as Argentina or Brazil), you may need to book a flight in advance. Apart from during peak periods and festivals (your guidebook will list these), you generally never have to book more than 24 hours in advance for a bus, boat, or train unless there is just one departure a day. In some countries, there are no schedules; transport simply leaves when it has enough passengers to make it economical for the company.

Bus

In most countries you travel, buses will be the most common form of your everyday transport. In some countries, there is just one class of bus, but in most, there are a variety of choices from the local "chicken bus" (so called because locals get on and off with their animals and market produce) to "express" (usually the fastest option with the fewest stops).

With express buses, you get an assigned seat number; there is air conditioning and usually a toilet on board. They usually show a DVD (most often a newly released action film, dubbed or subtitled) and may serve food and drinks. If they don't, they usually make a long stop for lunch or dinner at a roadside restaurant where there will be an opportunity also to buy snacks or bottled drinks. Most seats will recline, so many people take overnight buses as they save on a night's accommodation and mean you don't lose a day's travel by spending all day on a bus. If you travel at night, you arrive first thing in the morning and don't have the worry of trying to find your hostel in the dark and with all your belongings. An overnight bus does save a night's accommodation, but road accidents occur quite often in countries such as Bolivia. However, you may not have a choice as to when to travel. On certain routes in South America, the buses only travel overnight in order to bring vendors to the morning markets.

Local buses are more cramped, as people sit or stand in the aisle, and slower, since they stop regularly to pick up and drop off people on the side of the road. Vendors also come on board (pushing aside those in the aisle) to sell you everything from soft drinks, coconuts, and popcorn to belts and watches. It helps traveling in a pair on local buses to keep an eye on each other's valuables. Be wary of pickpockets. Your backpack will either be placed on the roof and securely fastened with rope (usually attached to a gas canister or bag of potatoes or vegetables) or placed at the back of the vehicle. Try to sit right next to your backpack or, at the very least, keep it constantly within eyesight.

So why travel on a "chicken bus" if it is cramped, slower, and potentially more stressful? Of course, it is much cheaper. But more important for me it is the experience of doing what the locals do and interacting with them. Most "chicken buses" are retired school buses from Canada and the USA that have been driven down to Central America, individually named, and beautifully decorated and painted. Hearing the gears crunch as the bus struggles up a hill and sharing a bench and exchanging pleasantries with a local is part of the experience. At the very least, it should be tried once! The toilet "facilities"– side of the road for men, women, and children alike – aren't for everyone, especially since the animals don't necessarily make a distinction!

Tips: Carry your own toilet paper and anti-bac, and take a jumper out of your rucksack for the aircon (in countries such as Venezuela, you'll be forgiven for thinking you're in a mobile refrigerator!). On night journeys, the overhead lights rarely work – use your head torch or reading lights that clip to your book.

Safety tips: Try to get a window seat that is on the side of the luggage compartment. Keep an eye out until the bus leaves and at stops that your bag isn't removed. Good bus companies will give you a receipt to retrieve your backpack from the luggage compartment, so all you need to do is look after your daysack. *Never put your daysack with valuables in the overhead compartment.* Instead, put one leg through one of the straps and loop it over your knee. It is not uncommon for bag slashers to put a razor blade through your daysack as you sleep, extract something, and leave at a stop before you've woken.

Other modes of transport are minibus and shared taxi. A minibus can be more expensive than a bus but also safer and more convenient for a number of reasons. They usually don't depart from the major bus stations (which are normally a hive of activity for pickpockets), can arrange pick up from your hostel, are fast, and make it easier to keep an eye on your bags. If there are a number of you, you can normally negotiate a group discount. A shared taxi (common in the Middle East) is extremely quick, if not slightly cramped, and leaves when it has enough passengers (four or five) unless you pay to charter it. If you decide to do this you may as well hire a driver, but arrange this through your hostel or hotel and be wary of the touts in the street. Aside from the safety aspect, you're less likely to be driven involuntarily to his cousin's carpet shop!

> Tip: When taking a local bus, minibus, or shared taxi, ask a local what they're paying to avoid a "gringo tax" – the operator or driver may attempt to rip you off if you are a foreigner or try to charge you extra for your bag.

Boat

Unless you decide to fly (not always an option), boats are your means of getting to and from islands. A boat may vary from a *panga* (Central American motorised fishing boat) or speed boat all the way up to a cruise liner or passenger ferry. With the former, your bags are hidden under a tarpaulin to keep them dry. The ride is often bumpy, wet, and, if you're prone to seasickness, quite uncomfortable. A passenger ferry, conversely, can be quite comfortable. You keep your bags with you, and there are toilets and kiosks on board. It is also easier to take photographs from a ferry. However, be aware that not all boats have life jackets, and some countries do not have impeccable safety records due to overloading and lack of lifeboats. If you feel uncomfortable before the boat departs, grab your bag and get off; you can't do anything once it's set off.

Train

Although departures will likely be less frequent than a bus, necessitating booking in advance, this can be one of the most enjoyable modes of transport. You can watch the world go by, move around, and stretch your legs. Although trains are generally more expensive than a bus, there may be different classes of carriage to suit each budget (but with differing levels of comfort). Try to avoid third class (for safety reasons) unless on the tightest of budgets. In Europe and Japan, rail passes can sometimes save you money but the latter must be purchased before you depart your home country. Apart from Japan, where trains are incredibly safe, never leave your bags unattended. If you are traveling on your own, ask a fellow traveler in your compartment to keep an eye on your backpack (take your daysack with you) whilst you visit the toilet. Many have sleeper berths or compartments, but be aware that these are rarely gender separated, so caution should be taken if you're female and traveling alone.

Plane

On shorter trips and/or across vast countries, pre-booking a flight may make sense – if you only have three or four weeks, spending two days on a boat or 36 hours on a bus eats into your time. If you book well in advance, the flight may not be that expensive. But generally speaking, traveling by air eats into your budget, and you learn more about a country going overland or by boat. On short internal flights, getting to and from two airports as well as having to check in hours before your flight may mean you don't save much time. Furthermore, internal flights aren't always flexible or refundable. However, each region has low-cost airlines (e.g., Air Asia in Asia or Easyjet/Ryanair in Europe) and some airlines offer air passes (e.g., LAN for South America) that can save you time and money. Peruse your guidebook's transport section. If you decide booking a flight works for you, be aware of flight safety records of local airlines.

On RTW flights, don't underestimate the effects of jet lag; take it easy the first few days after big time changes. Regardless of your flight type (internal or external), *always reconfirm your flight* online or by phone. Remember to take liquids greater than 100ml out your hand luggage. You don't want to buy and later replace your confiscated suntan lotion!

Car

If you're considering driving on your trip, you'll need an International Driving Permit before you leave. They are valid for 12 months, relatively inexpensive (from £5.5 in the UK) and readily available from post offices or motoring organisations. This permit is for use in conjunction with your driving licence, not in place of it, and both forms should be shown when hiring a car or stopped by the police.

Traveling by car gives you the freedom and flexibility not to be tied to a bus timetable or destination, and you can stop to take photos you wouldn't otherwise be able to by bus or train. However, it can be stressful driving in inner cities (no lanes and everyone for themselves in the Middle East!), and parking rules may not be immediately apparent. Local laws may not also be apparent. When hiring a car, automatics are generally more expensive than manual. Always check the insurance policy. If you're not a confident driver, don't do it, especially if you're nervous about driving on the other side of the road and tackling roundabouts.

Many travelers in Australia or New Zealand buy a car and sell it on at the end of their trip. Buy with people you know (and on similar timeframes), take it for a test drive, and don't indicate you're a short-termer as you may get ripped off. Hired car companies in the USA, for example, also need drivers to drive cars to a destination. You're responsible for the petrol and accommodation on route, but the car is otherwise free. Of course, if you want to lower accommodation costs, you can get a campervan or RV that comes equipped with sleeping quarters and a kitchenette, but you'll miss out on aspects of the backpacker trail that go along with staying in hostels.

Hitchhiking

I don't advocate hitchhiking from a safety perspective, but many people do it. New Zealand and Japan may be *relatively* safe places in which to hitch a ride, but the USA, Middle East, and South America may not be. Never hitch alone, especially if you are a woman, and try not to travel at night. Don't be pressured into getting into a car. Trust your gut instinct. If you are unsure, politely decline a lift. In some developing countries, it is customary to make a small payment to the driver.

Cycling

With cycling you can reach destinations off the bus routes and reach towns or villages less visited (indeed, it can be fun being the local celebrity!). Unlike buses, you can also stop to take pictures or go for a toilet break whenever you want. However, traveling by cycle requires a certain level of fitness and mechanical capability. Heat and altitude can be previously unknown factors, so you'll need the right equipment (e.g., a CamelBak for hydration, padded shorts, and waterproofs or thermals), and you'll need to be competent in carrying out basic repairs such as mending punctures. If in doubt what to take, there are various cycling organisations you can find on the internet that will give you great advice. Of course, many hostels and agencies organise cycling daytrips where you can rent or hire equipment, but if cycling is your main mode of transport, travel light and don't be stubborn. Load the bike onto public transport when you are tired – after all, things such as sunstroke and altitude sickness are not to be scoffed at.

Inner City

Taking a local bus or metro can be cheap, but beware of pickpockets in crowded spaces. Weaving through traffic in a motorised tuk-tuk or cyclo rickshaw can be fun, but agree the fare in advance and know that this method of transport is not without danger (accidents happen quite regularly). For the most part, inner-city sightseeing means a lot of walking. Look both ways when crossing roads. In some countries, taxis are relatively inexpensive. Always insist on them using the meter or agree the fare in advance, and make sure you are using a licensed taxi (see Personal Safety section).

Accommodation

Accommodation is one of the biggest day-to-day expenses on the road, so hostels are an obvious choice. The popular ones get booked up early, and most do during the high season or festivals (your guidebook will list the dates), so it pays to be proactive and book online. Other times of year, you can shop around looking for the best offer and can negotiate on price (especially if you are staying multiple nights), but this can be exhausting in the heat with your backpack on your back. Annotate a few on your guidebook that aren't too far apart when you get to a new town. It's perfectly acceptable to ask to see a room.

Hostels

To the first-time backpacker that has holidayed in hotels, the thought of a hostel may seem abhorrent. What can you expect? Before I answer that, the first thing to point out is that you're never in your room save for an afternoon siesta (which can be bliss after a day's sightseeing!) and at the end of the evening. Hostels usually have an array of types of room from dormitories ("dorms") to singles, twins, doubles, and privates (with three or four beds). Some rooms may be ensuite; otherwise, the hostel has shared facilities (either gender separated or communal with closed cubicles). Most have communal areas such as a living room with DVD player and board games, and some may have a bar with pool table or table-top football. Some have pets (anything from toucans to cats and dogs) – it can be fun to have a pet whilst away! Indeed, I've stayed in places where you can take the dog for a walk if you ask them at reception. Not all but some have kitchens where you can store things in the fridges (you have to label your food in a bag with your name and check-out date) and cook if you don't want to or can't afford to eat out. Some include breakfast in your accommodation rate, and some serve lunch or dinner for a price (barbecue nights, for example, are a good way of meeting people). Most have a few internet terminals (either included in the price or payable by the hour), and some have wifi for those with laptops (which may be good enough to check your email but not fast enough to upload photos!). I'll go through the different type of room.

Dorms

Apart from camping, dorms are the cheapest option available. They are normally arranged in bunk beds with ladders and can have as few as four individual beds per room, but most have between 8 and 16. The more beds there are, the cheaper the room; many of the smaller dormitories (4 to 6 beds) are ensuite – that is, the shower and toilet are only available for the occupants' use. Generally speaking, most dorms are mixed gender (so bring your pyjamas!) unless they specify female-only dorms (it's rare to have male-only dorms). The facilities will be basic, and there is a general lack of privacy (the exception to this is Japan, where some hostels have pull-across curtains, a plug socket and a reading lamp per bed), but it is a great way to meet other travelers. Common vexations are snorers, people coming in drunk and turning the lights on while being noisy, or people waking you up early with an alarm and zipping up bags for that early departure. That's essentially why you pay a small premium for a smaller dorm! But generally speaking, for the most part people are courteous and considerate.

What do you do with your valuables? Most hostels have safety deposit boxes at reception, but I advocate choosing a hostel with individual lockers. These will either be in the dorm room itself or in the corridor adjacent to the dorm and from my experience come in three sizes: small (can fit your camera, passport, money belt, and small items), medium (can fit the contents of your daypack) and large (can squeeze in your whole backpack if you pull out a few items). You'll need to use your own padlock (combination better than key, as you can lose the latter) or you can sometimes hire one at reception.

You'll pay a premium for a single room, but singles are great for those who are light sleepers and prefer some privacy yet still want the benefit of meeting people in the communal areas. A twin room will be cheaper per person than getting two singles (and can be cheaper than two dorm beds), so it is quite common for travelers to share one. The same applies to a double or private room, but don't travel with a partner or friends just to get your costs down (see Who Do You Go With? section). You won't have lockers in these rooms. Only the cleaner will have access to your room, but don't leave valuables lying around. Things do go missing. If you feel uncomfortable leaving your key at reception, insist on keeping it with you. For more advice on securing your valuables, please see the Safety/Accommodation section.

 Tip: Many hostels have paper-thin curtains and 100W light bulbs; for extra privacy you can secure a sarong or bed sheet to the curtains with hair clips.

Choosing a hostel based on word of mouth is best. If you meet someone who's just come from your next destination, ask where they stayed and whether they were happy. If a hostel is in your guidebook, you can bet the price has risen and/or the standard has slipped (once listed in a guidebook, they have guaranteed clientele so can hike the price or delay refurbishing). There are quite a few useful websites for searching hostels by arrival date and room type. They have feedback ratings, reviews (remember, one person's opinion is not necessarily definitive), photos, and descriptions of facilities available, such as breakfast, free wifi, security lockers, or airport pickup. Many charge a non-refundable deposit with the remainder payable on arrival. As aforementioned, it can be useful to book in advance if arriving late at night or in peak or holiday seasons, but the downside to booking in advance is that you lose your deposit if you're not happy on arrival. The most common websites are www.hostelworld.com and www.hostelbookers.com, although in Central and South America, www.hosteltrail.com is also useful as a destination guide.

Hotels

Hotel rooms are of course a little more expensive but are more comfortable, with most being ensuite and having mod cons such as aircon and satellite TV. They may better suit older people, couples, or families but are also appropriate for those who are wanting to splash out, have a swimming pool for a day, eat well, and escape dorm life and snorers. If you fall into this category, you'll lose the jovial atmosphere of a hostel living room and you're unlikely to have a kitchen for personal use, so save that expense for when you're tired of sightseeing and talking to random people and want to spend a bit of time in your *own* room.

At such times, even sitting in your room, munching popcorn, and watching the most dreadful satellite TV can be bliss!

Hotels will be listed in your guidebook mostly under the "mid-range" section and you can normally just turn up (they're less likely to be booked up in advance). For booking in advance, websites such as HotelsCombined.com or Kayak.com aggregate lodging options in a city.

Tips: If you've planned to stay somewhere you've spotted in a guidebook, a taxi driver on the way from the bus station may claim it is closed or no longer exists. You'll know they're lying to you if you've actually booked accommodation and paid a deposit online. Insist on going to your original destination. Such drivers are either trying to increase their fare on the meter or trying to get commission from the other place for introducing guests.

At hotels and hostels, the reception may not always be open 24 hours. If you're booking via a website and know you're arriving late, check whether it will be open and either book somewhere else or contact your first choice directly to make alternative arrangements. If you will be arriving early (i.e., before the room has been cleaned and you can check in), most places will allow you to store your bag in the luggage storage room or behind reception, but you do so at your own risk.

Once there, take a card from reception (most are written in English and the local language, so they are useful to show taxi drivers). Check the opening hours of reception and ask how you get access to the building after hours. Some places will give you a pin (write it on the back of the card!), and in others you simply bang on the door and apologetically stumble past the night watchman. Even the most experienced travelers have been caught out, not being able to get back into their hostel at night!

In some countries the hostel will insist on holding your passport until check out. It is better to try to use your laminated copy of your passport, as sometimes this will suffice. Don't walk off without either!

Some places offer tabs for snacks and drinks, with some operated on an honesty system. Don't swindle the hostel on the honesty system, as that is their livelihood, but equally, keep a mental note of what you've ordered for when the occasional deliberate accounting error occurs.

Apartments

If you think you're going to be somewhere for five nights or more, renting an apartment can be a cheaper and better alternative to a hostel. You may miss out on some of the benefits of a hostel, but this will be outweighed by the greater independence you will have, and self-catering can be a nice change from eating out. As well as searching online, ask in the Information Centre when you hit your destination how to go about renting an apartment, and keep an eye out for noticeboards around town.

Couchsurfing

This is a relatively new phenomenon whereby travelers can get a free bed, couch, or spot on the floor by staying with a local in various countries or cities. You need to enter a profile, and the website provides various levels of verification and allows users to rate and leave comments on traveler's profiles. Common sense should prevail here too: if you feel uneasy with your new "host," make a polite excuse and leave at the earliest opportunity.

Safety and Scams

Safety

Common sense and your gut instinct are your biggest asset whilst traveling. For example, let your hostel know where you're going and when you might return if you decide to hike alone; don't wade into the sea when drunk or when conditions are rough; and don't be tempted by drugs - being caught in possession can result in severe penalties, and you don't want to be doing this in a country where the law and language can be confusing. Some advice has already been included within Transport and Money, so this section covers mainly accommodation and personal safety. It also notes a few of the most common scams to be aware of.

Accommodation

When shown a room, check if the windows or shutters lock securely and try, if possible, to avoid the ground floor. Break-ins do occur even above ground level when there are adjacent balconies so don't leave your windows open.

Beach huts are great fun with their sand floors and proximity to the beach, but avoid ones that aren't lit up at night from the outside and try to stay in ones that have facilities onsite (e.g., a restaurant) and are attended by security guards. For as long as I have been traveling, from Koh Samui, Thailand, to Montanita, Ecuador, I've met people whose beach huts have been robbed at night whilst they're in town dining.

Some rooms padlock from the outside. If you are uncertain of the security, add your own padlock to that provided by the hostel. If you're only there for one or two nights, who cares if the cleaner can't access your room?

The novice backpacker often worries about being mugged in the street by a local and having items stolen but sadly, *more often than not, theft occurs from fellow backpackers.* For some reason people feel complacent and leave valuables lying about in dorm rooms as they think foreigners are less likely to steal than locals. But if you stop and think, you realize you wouldn't leave your wallet or camera in a coffee shop unattended! Many people charge their appliances in their dorm room, but it is better to do so in the communal areas within eyesight of you if you're in any doubt of your companions.

The two most common ways of backpacks being stolen are from the bus compartment or a storage room. You'll need to leave your backpack in a storage room from time to time, such as when sightseeing (after check-out) before an evening bus or whilst hiking. Never leave behind anything that you're worried about losing (including sentimental items) as insurance has limits for cover on individual items. Again, don't be overly paranoid, but try if you can to use a storage room that is locked and that gives you a receipt for your bag. However, trust your gut instinct as always. In many countries, bus terminals or tourist information centres have coin-operated lockers or storage rooms where you are given a receipt for your belongings. As a final word of advice, it is nice to have luxuries on the road, such as a laptop and speakers, but think hard what you want to take before you leave home if you're going to be doing a lot of outdoor activities and will be relying on storage rooms.

Tip: For the overly cautious, you can buy wire locks or lockable mesh covers that cover your whole rucksack. But both are relatively expensive, and the latter can weigh almost a kilogram (as a rule of thumb, a typical baggage weight limit for an airline is 20 kg). You fix it to an immovable object such as corner of bunk bed or the base of a sink. Another option is to padlock your backpack to an immovable object with a length of chain. This has always worked for me, but none of these methods are foolproof - if a thief wants your backpack, they'll take it. These methods just stop the opportunist who won't necessarily have the time to come back with a knife or bolt cutters. Indeed, there's also the age-old trick of making your backpack look as undesirable as possible. Try not to buy it at the last minute, and if you do, kick some dirt into it before it accrues mileage on your trip and naturally ages!

Personal Safety

As previously advised, as part of your pre-trip planning it is wise to check the FCO website but check again on arrival to see if anything has changed. The Dangers and Annoyances section of your guidebook is always relevant, but new scams evolve. Your hostel workers are a great source of advice. They see travelers come and go every day and will be aware of guests who have had to contact embassies, police stations, or hospitals, so ask them whether you need a taxi at night and whether there are parts of the city you should avoid, etc.

Don't make yourself a target. Don't wear an expensive watch (leave it at home!) or excessive amounts of jewellery, and try not to flash your wealth. Carrying a camera around your neck and listening to an iPod may be normal in some parts of the world, but those on subsistence wages will see great value in "borrowing" your belongings.

Always use licensed taxis. Insist on using the meter or agree the fare in advance. Don't share taxis with strangers, especially at night. Be wary of road traffic as a pedestrian (look both ways). Try to keep your drink with you at all times to avoid your drink being spiked, which can result in robbery or, worse still, rape.

Women Travelers

As mentioned in the Who Do You Go With? section, it is quite common to set off on your own, but the beautiful thing about traveling is that you rarely are alone. It is perfectly common for women to travel by themselves; however, extra caution need be applied in male-dominated Muslim countries, India, parts of Africa, and areas of South America where sexism is rife. Take precautions too when traveling at night or by taxis unaccompanied (i.e., book through your hostel). Some female travelers advocate wearing a fake wedding ring to deter untoward advances, but I've seen these act as an incentive for the prowler in some countries! Better to avoid eye contact and conversation and keep walking when approached in the street. Local women will be your proxy – if they do, dress conservatively, avoid excessive make-up, and wear a one-piece or t-shirt at the beach. Impressions are gained from Western films – even drinking on your own can be seen as the green light for an approach or suggestive of promiscuity. If your polite rebuttals are ignored and you feel at all nervous, don't hesitate to raise your voice. Most men will be wary of an audience and back away.

 Tip: Several brands of pull-pin activating personal alarms worn as pendants are available on the internet. They are inexpensive and light.

Scams

Even the most experienced travelers get scammed from time to time, but it helps being aware of the most common tricks. Travelers are great storytellers (exaggerators?), you will find. If you meet someone who has been tricked or robbed, pay attention to how. The below list is not comprehensive, since fraudsters are becoming increasingly inventive, but these methods have been around for some time:

When crossing borders by land, change the bulk of your unused money at a foreign exchange office *beforehand* but leave enough money for your bus *on the other side* to exchange with a moneychanger; then use an ATM at your destination. If it's a new country you're entering and you've never seen the currency before, it can be hard to tell if your acquired currency is genuine or not, especially when there is an old currency that has become defunct. If you can, ask a local person crossing simultaneously whether you could see what one of their notes looks like. Most moneychangers will accept US dollars, so it's always useful to have some bills. The problem is not just confined to border crossings. A shop owner or restaurant can just as easily give you counterfeit notes as change. Your guidebook should normally describe the currency, so have a close look at your notes when you first acquire them.

Sometimes a restaurant owner will try giving you the change for a smaller note (e.g., change for 10 instead of a 20). When you question it, they will be extremely confident and try to put doubt in your mind. As soon as you say "I *thought* it was a 10," they'll prey on your uncertainty and say that you're not even sure yourself. Be firm and they'll apologise for the confusion. Or, if dining with someone else, ensure that you are both there when you receive the change before one of you heads off to the bathroom.

A quite common bus station trick is that someone "spills" something on you and then offers to "help you" wipe it off. They've actually thrown it on you, and an accomplice will be attempting to pickpocket you whilst you're distracted. If this happens, walk away immediately and inspect your clothes after – you're only wearing traveler's clobber anyway!

Another trick involves a passerby dropping something on the floor. You go to pick it up for them, as an honest citizen, but when you look up, they're gone. A policeman across the road grabs you before you've had the choice to inspect what's been dropped. The policeman will catch you red-handed with a small parcel of drugs and say you'll need to come to the police station or pay an on-the-spot fine and relieve you of cash.

If traveling alone, be wary of accepting food or drink from strangers on public transport (it's fine to try foods before purchasing in a food market); you may wake up drowsy later, relieved of your belongings.

Post-Trip

Coming Home

Traveling can be one of the most rewarding things you do in your lifetime, so coming home can be a hard transition. It is difficult to go *from* flip-flops, daily sightseeing, and no particular schedule *to* shoes, sitting still and routine. Don't get back immediately before university starts or before you have to go back to work. Allow yourself time to settle back in and catch up with people, and set aside enough money to dine out a few times or have your favourite takeaway. When catching up with people, don't be surprised that your friends aren't 100 per cent interested in your trip or stories. They may have commenced cohabiting, gotten married or had a baby whilst *you* were away. Work is work, whatever their new circumstances and travel stories just rub it in! Your mum is usually one exception to the rule, though.

There are many good things about returning. It may be fun exploring your old town again, and you can appreciate the small things so much better: not padlocking things, sitting still, and lying on a sofa alone. Sleeping in your own bed and eating familiar foods can be bliss. Best of all, you are with people who have known you for a long time, and you can communicate with them face-to-face or by phone and no longer via instant messenger or Skype. In fact, after a long trip, even that dreaded visit to the dentist will be bliss – no matter how many times you floss or brush your teeth on the road, you'll be itching for a clean from the hygienist!

A few weeks after your return, however, the euphoria of catching up with people may subside when you are faced with "What now?" questions and realise that sitting still can sometimes be more expensive than you think. When dealing with post-travel blues, it helps to stay active and get out of the house early in the day. Sign up for a gym if you can afford it or go for a run in a park. Have a CV/resume updated before you go on your trip. Even if you don't have work lined up, getting jobs through a temp agency will help allay short-term monetary concerns and also give you a structure to the week. Have another destination in mind you can go to on holiday when you return to full-time work. In the short term, staying in touch with other travelers you met helps, as they can relate more to your experiences.

But whatever you do, pat yourself on the back and think of your achievements: you saw some amazing things, met some great people, and got back in one piece. Get some photos enlarged and hang them as prints as a reminder of your trip and inspiration for your next when you return to work. Most importantly, however, learn from your trip! If work was the be-all and end-all before your trip, be proactive in organising your spare time and find time for that new hobby or sport when back at work again. Okay, it's not hiking, snorkelling, or relaxing in a hammock, but getting events in the diary (weekends away, concerts, etc.) gives you something to look forward to and will make you a happier individual.

About the Author

Since a gap year 16 years ago, Mark James Vang has undertaken trips from two weeks to 13 months continuously. A tally of 72 countries to date and counting includes trips around Africa, Asia, Australasia, Europe, the Americas and the Middle East. He currently resides in London.

Index

Lightning Source UK Ltd.
Milton Keynes UK
UKOW04f2303111213

222869UK00001B/146/P

9 781483 404769